FABER NEW P(

IN THE SAME SERIES

Elaine Beckett

for Sue
Elaine B.

ff

FABER & FABER

First published in 2016
by Faber & Faber Ltd
Bloomsbury House
74–77 Great Russell Street
London WC1B 3DA

Typeset by Hamish Ironside
Printed in England by Abbeystar

ACKNOWLEDGEMENTS

Thanks to editors at the Bridport Prize Anthology, Templar Poetry,
Bloodaxe Books and Flagon Press, who have published some of these poems;
to Raving Beauties, Annie Freud, the Cattistock Poets and Some Bridport Poets;
to Martha Sprackland and Matthew Hollis; to Greta Stoddart
and members of her Poetry School seminar groups.

A CIP record for this book
is available from the British Library

ISBN 978–0–571–33039–3

2 4 6 8 10 9 7 5 3 1

Contents

Melting

There was very little left on the marble slab:
a few tubs of prawns, a kipper.
Fishmonger, first to launch in,
said he'd wanted to throw something at the telly
last night, turns out we'd both wanted to
and we'd both rewound

to check if Met Office man
had really had a smile on his face
as he pointed to the melting ice.

Then fishmonger told me he used to be a journalist
and I said I'd like to buy his kipper;
for you, he mouthed, the kipper will be just two pounds.

I looked at him, he looked at me –
we tacitly agreed to extend the conversation
while he sloshed about with his bucket
and I enjoyed the rain
that was coming down like a veil
between us, and the passers-by.

Kensington

Tell us how the dinner went –
did you have it in your new kitchen?
Did you get someone in?

Yes, I got someone in.

It was quite awkward in a way –
you see we've no splashbacks
now that it's sleek.

Norfolk Winter '72

I'd said fuck a couple of times too many at a party
when everyone else was saying bloody

and that was it – he wanted me
no matter I belonged to someone else.

Next day he borrowed a van, drove to the cottage
and asked for me;

stared straight at you in the firelight, under the low ceiling,
fearing you'd attack him with the poker.

Like silent stags, you each compared the other's coat,
heads almost touching;

how deep was the fur, was it really from Afghanistan,
had the other even heard of Philip Roth?

So of course I packed my baskets and moved into his –
any flower girl worth her candles would have done the same.

The Woman Who Cries
by Pablo Picasso

It arrived in a clean white envelope
stamped Rotterdam,
as if he were trying to gain perspective.

I'd hoped for a neutral image –
a canal, a piece of Delft,
but the message read:

don't be La Femme Qui Pleure –
and underneath, he'd underlined the title.

So I turned the card over and there she was:
fractured, pitiful, a red-and-blue lifeboat lodged
in her hair, driven mad by her own salt waters.

I kept her close to me for days
until I began to feel grateful,

grateful for knowing such a man,
a man who could match me to a painting
that summarised the trouble we were in.

Killer Whale

I'd switched on out of nothing better to do.
Soon I'm watching a boy in a wet suit,
tugged by his foot by a black and white whale

then plunged at speed
to the bottom of the SeaWorld lagoon,
because that's where this is happening – in Florida.

His lungs are about to burst.
Next it's the turn of the trainee attendant
who's run out of fish;

she hasn't blown her whistle quite right,
the orca doesn't like it, so *she* gets dragged under,
tossed in the air and savaged.

Then somebody asks the obvious question –
why do they keep him?
Next they show him lying still, in the practice pool;

fin flipped over, motionless,
his lonely penis being stroked for its sperm
and the trainers explain how they need it

to keep the whole operation going, but someone
points out they are breeding psychopaths
and I think why on *earth* am I watching this?

Later that week I dream I'm a bear;
completely protected in thick brown fur,
at ease with myself in the wild.

Dreaming of the Professor
Who Gave Me the Sack

As the room was opening to other rooms,
he led me out across a courtyard

to a house with ragged books and guests
and remnants of conversations

that people had given up on.
We drifted past the usual cardboard pillars

to a half-dark open space
where he laid me on his sheets, still warm

from someone else, and I thought – okay
so far, yes – then turned my head

to find right next to me a bra,
just as she'd left it, before he'd laid her down.

How on Earth Would We Have Managed

The waves were *this* high

    that smuggler is a good man
    he gave us a discount

a good man? when the wind was from the north?
the waves were *this* high, people warned us not to use him

    how can you be sure?

how can we trust? Maybe the smuggler *is* a good man
look – there are people on the beach right now, terrified

    (distraught)

everyone knows you don't cross when the wind is from the
    north . . .

    we had to take a chance
    we've only so much money left

    trust me
    that smuggler – he's a good man.

We could have drowned.

2

The waves were big, bigger than I thought they'd be

  it was touch-and-go at times

a lot of the time,

  you are right. To be honest I didn't think we'd make it

neither did I, but we are here now

  yes, we are here.

Those people on the beach, the ones who've just arrived
they look terrified

  just like we were, maybe we shouldn't have risked it?

if there'd been another way, we wouldn't.

  Let's not blame one another, we are here now

and we're alive.

A Mess of Strangers

You don't need to know about the fifty minute ride
with a driver who poured his heart out about Bach,
      one partita in particular,

leaning back to give me his phone so I could watch
a clip of him practising the piece in Stepney,
      while he turned onto the Euston Road.

I thought is he having me on?
Is this one of those keyboards that automatically plays partitas?
      Soon I'll be feeling claustrophobic

in a stationary vehicle in an underpass while Glen here
goes on and on about the crash that just happened
      on the M25 with this music

that's perfectly suited to both topics, though
because I'm on my way to a difficult encounter
      with a woman I've never met before,

about to entrust her with a lifetime's secret,
it is actually quite good I am watching this stranger
      play a partita I hardly ever play

while he drives me to a street I've never been to before.
Far harder to have had to worry
      about the reason I am going there

in a silent taxi, or worse still, a cab in which
the only thing to listen to is a story about a lorry
      crossing a central reservation.

Small Puffin Jug

This morning,
I decided to open the boxes
we never meant to leave
for quite so long,

and there you were, our puffin jug –
all plump and optimistic,
ready to start over,
be filled.

So I went to the garden,
picked marigolds,
laid a table.

Elizabeth David's Instructions for Crêpes Dentelles

You tell me the amount of butter I should melt is 'infinitesimal' –

I know that in your kitchen it would never scorch, smoke
or blacken a pan which must be heavy and iron;
greased 'very very lightly'.

Now I must stir the eggs, flour, sugar and rum with your pinch
of salt, and the weight of all this in more melted butter
until 'very very smooth'

though I do not understand how to weigh melted butter,
so it may not be right.

You mention only now, in passing, that this recipe differs
from other pancake mixtures –

I must keep a quarter pint of milk tepid, add it 'very very gradually'
until the batter is about the consistency of 'very thick cream'.

I wonder how thick the cream was in 1960, read of your visit to
an old established restaurant in Strasbourg
while dipping my finger in to test;

apparently the place was 'so discreet as to be hardly recognisable
as a restaurant', until they brought you the bill,

how you followed the foie gras with whole baby chickens –
grilled, coated with breadcrumbs, parsley, chopped hard-boiled egg
and noisette butter –

how a little bowl of caraway seeds came with your Munster –
a strong, rich, creamy-textured cheese which at the right stage of
ripeness, you explain, is 'one of the great cheeses of France'

and that after this, delicate pancakes were served,
each stuffed with a kirsch-flavoured cream.

I notice my pan – how the air above it hovers.

Rehearsal for a Night-time Scene with Thunder

Wake up slow, reach for his hand
it won't be there,

try to fathom who you are, and why
then leave the bed,

pad across the room,
negotiate the eight foot six TV (in the shape of a guitar)

now try to part the drapes, they'll smell of money,
place your palms on the cool glass,

search the vertical drop,
the wet dazzle;

a curve in the curtain on your left –
it will shift a moment,

the moment you begin to make him out;
naked but for headphones and a mic,

your semi-jaded-angel-engineer,
gesturing you must not make a sound –

now wait real still while he records his track:
rain plunges eleven floors down to patched-up tarmac.

Hollywood Hotel

After the guys had got their awards
we understood each other's need
to sag back in our seats
and breathe out.

The matching of ties, tuxedos,
cufflinks, shoes, belts, haircuts
and moustachios
had all been worth it –

for there they were, up on the stage
holding their crystal balls.
A woman beside me leaned in to whisper:
I just want to say how natural you look.

For Roy

Twice round the block in sheeting rain,
up windy hill, in all weathers
he'd parade the rows of bungalows

with a smile, or a kind word,
as if he were in charge
and in a way he was;

first to notice if lights were still on
beyond half past ten, or someone had parked
by the blackthorn hedge,

he'd store it all up for a conversation
with anyone, anyone willing to pass
the cold time of day.

Jean is at her window trying to make sense of it,
how it could have happened like that,
all of a sudden, like that.

Something Pink

A flurry of sleet,
blowing in from God knows where –
or is it hail

spatters the cellophane
that holds my six bright tulips,
cheerful with possibilities.

Something pink
to put next to the absence
on the mantelpiece.

Sometime This Month

By the hedge at the end of the lane
where the gate has swung open,
a may tree will bloom;

five petals to each milk flower, pink-
tipped with stamens: a thousand buds
by the hedge at the end of the lane,

waiting for light.
Even in the shadow of nettles
a may tree will bloom

if the time is right; boys walking home
will be struck by the stink of it down
by the hedge, at the end of the lane

where they linger to check out their calls
and to text – that's where
a may tree will bloom,

and girls will let their shoulders show,
and stop to chat about their legs
by the hedge, at the end of the lane,
a may tree will bloom.